OUR PLANET IS 4.5 BILLION YEARS OLD, and has seen many different types of living creatures. Life on Earth began with single-cell organisms, and burst into a diverse multitude in an event called the 'Cambrian explosion' about 500 million years ago. Dinosaurs, woolly mammoths and sabre-toothed tigers are some of the fascinating creatures that lived on Earth but which are now extinct.

In their place, around 7 billion humans now live on Earth.

YOUR HOME PLANET

Earth's inner core is **6,000 °C HOT.**

That's hotter than the surface of the Sun!

CRUST
30–50 km thick

MANTLE
2,900 km thick

LIQUID OUTER CORE
2,250 km thick

SOLID INNER CORE
1,200 km thick

---

10 km

8 km

6 km

4 km

2 km

8.8 km
Peak of Mount Everest

SEA LEVEL

2 km

4 km — **3.7 km deep**
Average ocean floor

6 km

8 km

10 km

11 km deep
Deepest known ocean depth

12 km — **12 km deep**
Deepest man-made hole in the Kola Peninsula in Russia

2027

2028

2029

2030
Possible first manned mission to Mar

GREENHOUSE EFFECT

Some solar radiation is absorbed and stored by the Earth's atmosphere, causing it to warm up.

Some solar radiation is reflected by the Earth and the atmosphere.

Solar radiation passes through the clear atmosphere.

CLOUD TYPES IN THE TROPOSPHERE

8 km

CIRRUS

6 km

CIRROSTRATUS

ALTOSTRATUS

4 km

ALTOCUMULUS

2 km

STRATUS

CUMULUS

0 km

nned launch of JUICE to
plore the icy moons of Jupiter

THERMOSPHERE

MESOSPHERE

Above its surface, Earth is wrapped in a blanket of air called THE ATMOSPHERE.

It is held in place by Earth's gravity and keeps the temperature down below comfortable for us. Nearly three-quarters of the atmosphere is made of nitrogen gas, and most of the rest is the oxygen that we breathe.

STRATOSPHERE

TROPOSPHERE

Earth's atmosphere gets thinner and thinner the higher you go.

HERE ARE FOUR MAIN LAYERS OF THE ATMOSPHERE.

The **troposphere** stretches to a height of about 10 km. This is the layer of the atmosphere we live in. The **stratosphere** stretches from 10 to 50 km above Earth's surface. The temperature here ranges from 60 °C to 18 °C. The **mesosphere** (50 km to 85 km) can get as cold as -90 °C. The upper main layer of the atmosphere is the **thermosphere**, which stretches hundreds of kilometres into space.

The stratosphere contains a very special gas called **ozone**. This gas acts like nature's sunscreen. It stops too many of the Sun's **ultraviolet (UV) rays** getting through to the planet. Pollution from factories, cars and fires can make the ozone very thin, which means more harmful rays reach the surface of the Earth, causing sunburn.

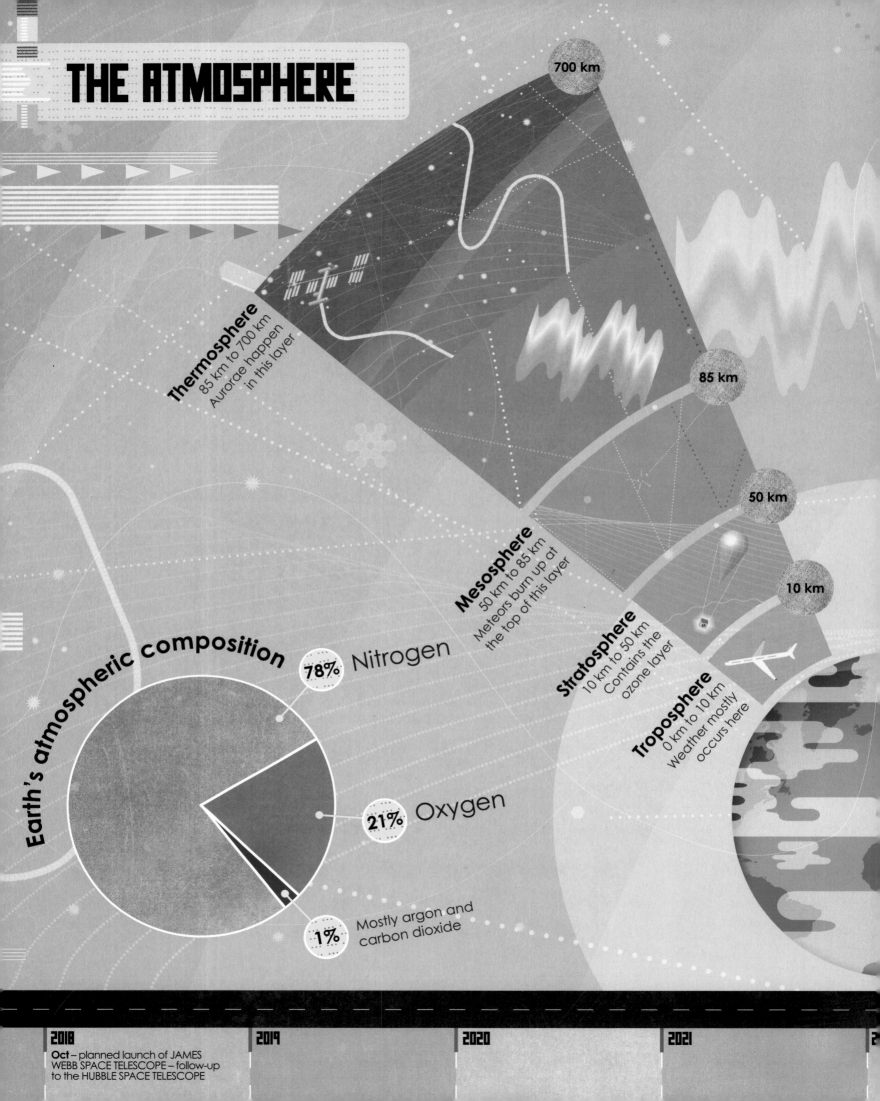

THE ATMOSPHERE

700 km

85 km

50 km

10 km

Thermosphere
85 km to 700 km
Aurorae happen
in this layer

Mesosphere
50 km to 85 km
Meteors burn up at
the top of this layer

Stratosphere
10 km to 50 km
Contains the
ozone layer

Troposphere
0 km to 10 km
Weather mostly
occurs here

Earth's atmospheric composition

78% Nitrogen

21% Oxygen

1% Mostly argon and
carbon dioxide

Oct – planned launch of JAMES
WEBB SPACE TELESCOPE – follow-up
to the HUBBLE SPACE TELESCOPE

The different crews of astronauts on board the ISS have eaten a total of more than

25,000 meals so far.

There are more than **13 km of wires** for providing electricity to the ISS.

52 computers are used to control the ISS.

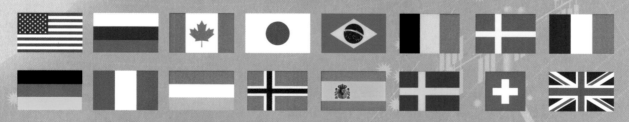

USA, Russia, Canada, Japan, Brazil, Belgium, Denmark, France, Germany, Italy, the Netherlands, Norway, Spain, Sweden, Switzerland and the United Kingdom **ALL CONTRIBUTE TO THE ISS.**

2014
Aug – first spacecraft to orbit a comet (Churyumov-Gerasimenko)
12 Nov – PHILAE probe lands on a comet

2015
Jan – NEW HORIZONS flyby of Pluto
March – DAWN – first spacecraft to orbit a dwarf planet (Ceres)

2016

2017
Planned launch of BEPICOLOMBO mission to orbit Mercury

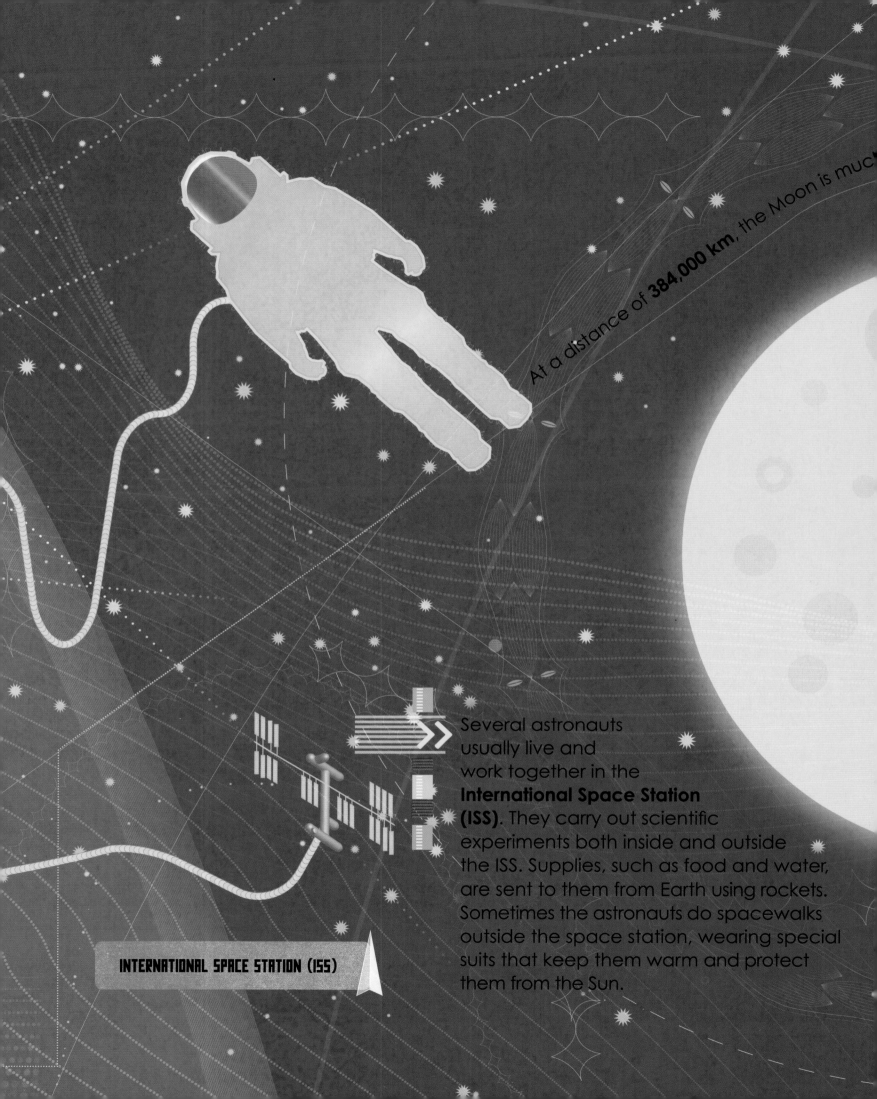

At a distance of **384,000 km**, the Moon is muc^{...}

Several astronauts usually live and work together in the **International Space Station (ISS)**. They carry out scientific experiments both inside and outside the ISS. Supplies, such as food and water, are sent to them from Earth using rockets. Sometimes the astronauts do spacewalks outside the space station, wearing special suits that keep them warm and protect them from the Sun.

INTERNATIONAL SPACE STATION (ISS)

...her away from Earth than the International Space Station.

While a rocket can take astronauts to the ISS in just 6 hours, in the late 1960s and early 1970s it took 3 days for the Apollo missions to fly astronauts to the Moon!

The Moon's surface is covered with rocks and dark grey dust. There are many large craters on the Moon that formed when comets and asteroids crashed there billions of years ago. Some of the ice from these comets is still on the Moon's surface today! There is no water, atmosphere, wind or life on the Moon.

For a spacecraft to be launched into orbit around Earth, it needs to travel at an amazing 40,000 km/h. Thousands of man-made satellites orbit just a few hundred kilometres above the Earth, as do the Hubble Space Telescope and the ISS.

ORBITING EARTH

ISS has more **living space** than a 6-bed house.

Its speed in orbit is
27,760 km/h –
that means the ISS travels
a total distance each
day that is almost
the same as going to
the Moon and back!

15,000

20,000

10,000

25,000

5,000

0

30,000

ISS weighs more than 320 cars!

March – MESSENGER –
first spacecraft to orbit Mercury
July – DAWN spacecraft goes into
orbit around asteroid Vesta

6 Aug – CURIOSITY rover lands on Mars
Aug – VOYAGER 1 crosses into
interstellar space

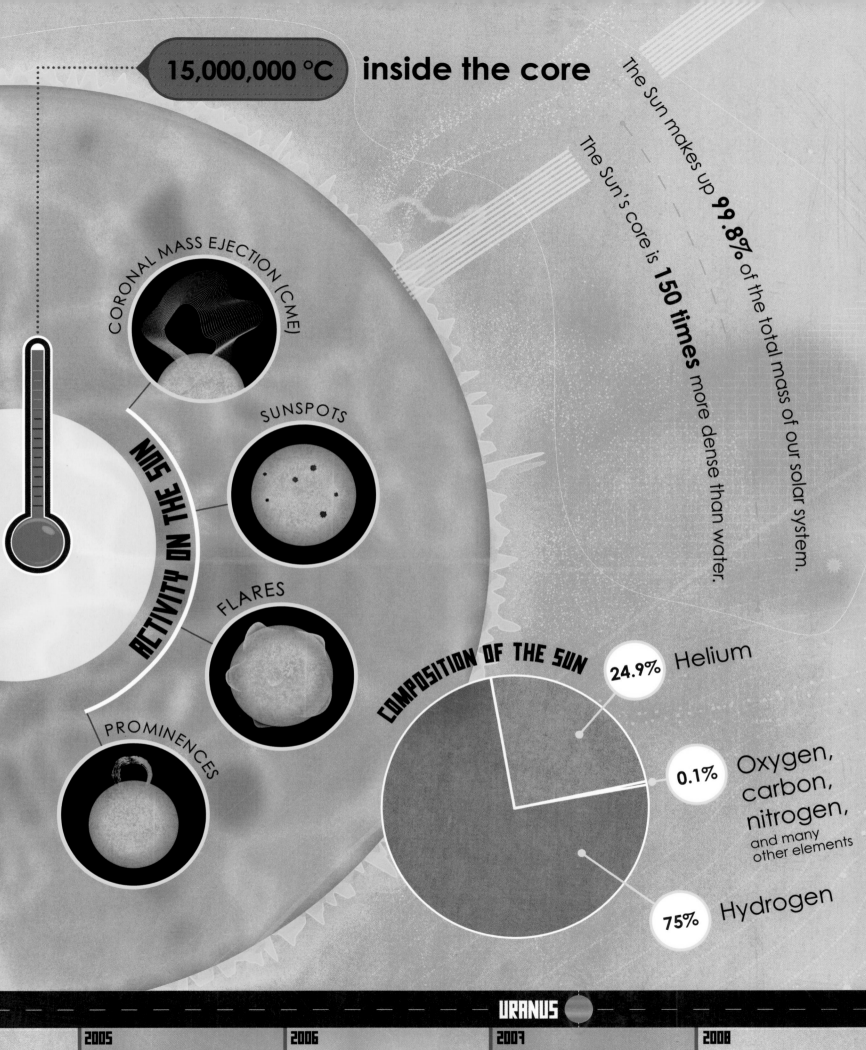

15,000,000 °C inside the core

The Sun makes up **99.8%** of the total mass of our solar system.

The Sun's core is **150 times** more dense than water.

ACTIVITY ON THE SUN

CORONAL MASS EJECTION (CME)

SUNSPOTS

FLARES

PROMINENCES

COMPOSITION OF THE SUN

24.9% Helium

0.1% Oxygen, carbon, nitrogen, and many other elements

75% Hydrogen

URANUS

2005
14 Jan – HUYGENS probe lands on Saturn's moon Titan

2006
March – MARS RECONNAISSANCE ORBITER goes into orbit around Mars

2007

2008

June
CASSINI
spacecraft
arrives at Saturn

THE SUN IS OUR NEAREST STAR

and the centre of our solar system. Like all stars, the Sun is a gigantic ball of hydrogen and helium gas. Nuclear energy generated in the Sun's core keeps it hot and shining.

Our Sun is 150 MILLION KM from Earth.

Our Sun looks bigger and brighter than the other stars in the night sky because it is much closer to us. **The next nearest star to the Sun is nearly 270,000 times further away!**

Sometimes there are tremendous explosions on the surface of the Sun called FLARES.

Huge blasts of radiation and gas burst out of the Sun during a flare. When this electrified gas strikes Earth, it can cause beautiful light shows in our planet's atmosphere called **aurorae**. Flares and other storms from the Sun can also harm satellites and astronauts when they are in orbit around the Earth.

THE SUN

CHROMOSPHERE
2,000 km thick
The outer layer of the
Sun's atmosphere.

PHOTOSPHERE
500 km thick
Energy radiates through here.

CONVECTIVE ZONE
200,000 km thick
Flowing currents of gas
carry energy to the outside
of the Sun's atmosphere.

RADIATIVE ZONE
350,000 km thick
The visible surface of the Sun.

CORE
150,000 km radius
The Sun's nuclear energy is
generated here.

5,500 °C surface temperature

1.3 million Earths
would fit inside the Sun

2000
eb – NEAR SHOEMAKER –
rst spacecraft to orbit an
steroid (Eros)

2001
12 Feb – NEAR SHOEMAKER makes
first landing on an asteroid
28 April – first tourist in space

2002

2003
Aug – SPRITZER SPACE TELESCOPE
launched
Dec – MARS EXPRESS goes into orbit
around Mars

2004
Jan – SPIRIT and
OPPORTUNITY
rovers land on
Mars

MERCURY

Radius = **2,439 km**

Distance from Sun = **57,910,000 km**

Time to orbit the Sun = **88 Earth days**

Rotation period = **59 Earth days**

Satellites (moons) = **0**

VENUS

Radius = **6,052 km**

Distance from Sun = **108,200,000 km**

Time to orbit the Sun = **225 Earth days**

Rotation period = **243 Earth days**

Satellites (moons) = **0**

WEATHER FORECASTS

MERCURY
No storms, cloud, wind or rain. Watch out for a huge drop in temperature from day to night!

VENUS
Total unbroken cloud cover from horizon to horizon. Crushing pressure and incredibly hot. Chance of acid rain in the clouds, but it won't reach the ground!

EARTH
Anything is possible: rain, storms, wind, clouds or sunshine.

MARS
Occasional light winds, but chance of huge dust storms that may turn the air orange!

GIANT MOUNTAIN

Olympus Mons on Mars is the largest mountain in the solar system. It is nearly 25 km high – nearly three times the height of Mount Everest.

Olympus Mons

Mount Everest

1996

1997
4 July – PATHFINDER rover lands on Mars
Sept – MARS GLOBAL SURVEYOR – goes into orbit around Mars

1998
20 Nov – Launch of the first ISS module

1999
Sept – CHANDRA X-RAY OBSERVATORY launched

OUR SOLAR SYSTEM HAS 8 PLANETS,

as well as thousands of smaller objects, such as moons, comets and asteroids. It formed around 5 billion years ago out of a huge cloud of swirling gas and dust. The planets closest to the Sun are rocky, with solid surfaces you could stand on.

VENUS is about the size of the Earth, but it is wrapped in a very thick atmosphere. It traps enough heat to make Venus's surface so hot it could melt lead!

MERCURY is closest to the Sun and the smallest planet. Its grey surface is covered in craters, a lot like Earth's moon.

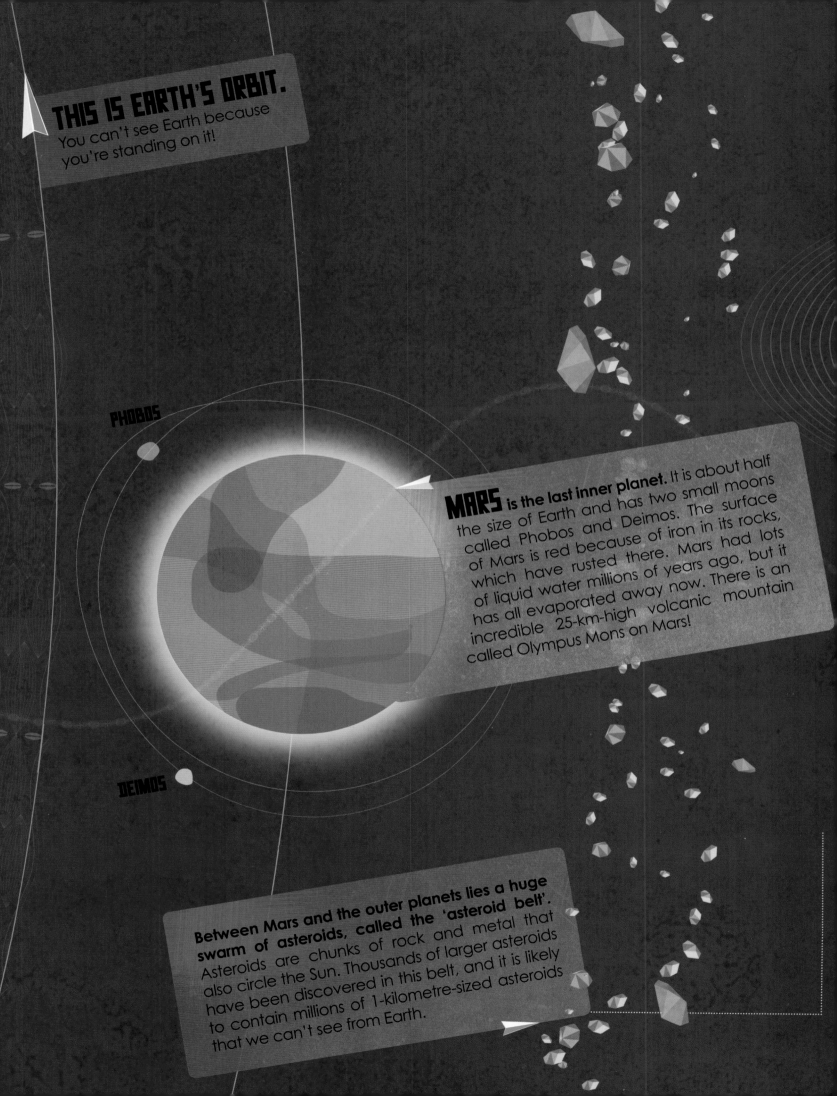

THIS IS EARTH'S ORBIT.
You can't see Earth because
you're standing on it!

PHOBOS

DEIMOS

MARS is the last inner planet. It is about half the size of Earth and has two small moons called Phobos and Deimos. The surface of Mars is red because of iron in its rocks, which have rusted there. Mars had lots of liquid water millions of years ago, but it has all evaporated away now. There is an incredible 25-km-high volcanic mountain called Olympus Mons on Mars!

Between Mars and the outer planets lies a huge swarm of asteroids, called the 'asteroid belt'. Asteroids are chunks of rock and metal that also circle the Sun. Thousands of larger asteroids have been discovered in this belt, and it is likely to contain millions of 1-kilometre-sized asteroids that we can't see from Earth.

THE INNER PLANETS

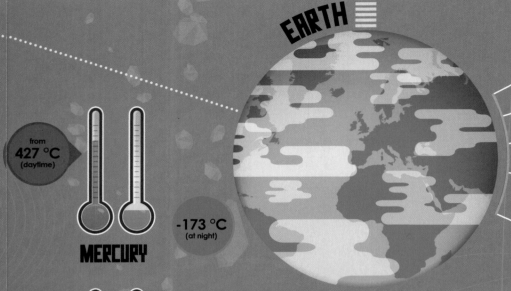

EARTH

Radius = **6,378 km**

Distance from Sun = **149,600,000 km**

Time to orbit the Sun = **365 Earth days**

Rotation period = **23 hours and 56 minutes**

Satellites (moons) = **1**

MARS

Radius = **3,397 km**

Distance from Sun = **227,940,000 km**

Time to orbit the Sun = **687 Earth days**

Rotation period = **24 hours and 37 minutes**

Satellites (moons) = **2**

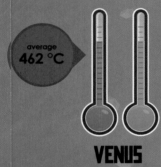

MERCURY

from **427 °C** (daytime)

-173 °C (at night)

VENUS

average **462 °C**

average **462 °C**

EARTH

58 °C hottest regions

-88 °C cold spots

MARS

-5 °C summer

-87 °C winter

ATMOSPHERES

Mars – thin: mostly carbon dioxide (95%) and a little nitrogen

Earth – thick: mostly nitrogen (78%) and oxygen

Mercury – none

Venus – thick: mostly carbon dioxide (98%), and a little nitrogen and sulphuric acid

1992

1993

1994

1995
7 Dec – GALILEO arrives at Jupiter
Dec – SOHO – solar observatory launched

SATURN

Radius = **58,232 km**

Distance from Sun
= **1,433,000,000 km**

Time to orbit the Sun
= **10,756 Earth days**

Rotation period
= **10.5 hours**

Satellites (moons) = **62**

JUPITER

Radius = **69,911 km**

Distance from Sun
= **778,500,000 km**

Time to orbit the Sun
= **4,333 Earth days**

Rotation period
= **10 hours**

Satellites (moons) = **67**

X?

HOW MANY EARTHS FIT INSIDE?

Jupiter – **1,321**

Saturn – **763**

Uranus – **63**

Neptune – **57**

WIND SPEED

JUPITER
635 km/h

SATURN
1,800 km/h

URANUS
900 km/h

NEPTUNE
2,100 km/h

In comparison, the maximum wind speeds reached (briefly) inside a tornado or powerful hurricane on Earth is about 300 km/h.

1987

1988

1989
25 Aug – VOYAGER 2 – arrives at Neptune

1990
24 April – HUBBLE SPACE TELESCOPE launched
10 Aug – MAGELLAN spacecraft arrives at Venus

1991

JUPITER is the king of the planets. We can see coloured layers of clouds high in its atmosphere that make swirling patterns as the planet spins around very quickly. There is also a giant storm called the Great Red Spot. It is twice the size of the Earth and has been raging for more than 300 years.

NEPTUNE is so far away it takes about 165 Earth years to complete an orbit around the Sun. It has the strongest winds anywhere in the solar system.

URANUS is smaller than Saturn and is blue because of methane gas in its atmosphere. It spins on its side and has vertical rings.

SATURN has beautiful bright rings made of chunks of ice. The rings are more than 280,000 km across but only 1 km thick. It has 62 moons including Titan, the only known satellite to have its own atmosphere.

Beyond the asteroid belt where the temperatures are much lower, giant planets formed. They are mostly made of hydrogen and helium, and have rings around them and dozens of moons. These giant planets are mostly made of liquefied gas. They don't have a surface so you could never land on one!

Beyond Neptune lie huge numbers of small, icy worlds including the dwarf planets Pluto, Haumea, Makemake and Eris. At almost 120 times the distance between the Earth and the Sun, we reach the solar system's edge, called the heliopause. Beyond it we no longer feel the effects of the Sun, **and we are heading into the space between the stars.**

THE OUTER PLANETS

URANUS

Radius = **25,362 km**

Distance from Sun
= **2,871,000,000 km**

Time to orbit the Sun
= **30,687 Earth days**

Rotation period
= **17 hours**

Satellites (moons) = **27**

NEPTUNE

Radius = **24,622 km**

Distance from Sun
= **4,499,000,000 km**

Time to orbit the Sun
= **60,190 Earth days**

Rotation period
= **16 hours**

Satellites (moons) = **14**

RINGS

JUPITER

SATURN

NEPTUNE

URANUS

30 kg = 71 kg

GRAVITY is different on each planet.

For example, if you weigh 30 kg on Earth,
then your weight on Jupiter will be 71 kg!

1983

1984

1985

1986
Jan – VOYAGER 2 – arrives at Uranus
20 Feb – MIR space station launched

There may be 100,000,000,000,000,000,000,000 STARS
(one thousand million) in the Universe!

Here are some star constellations visible from Earth:

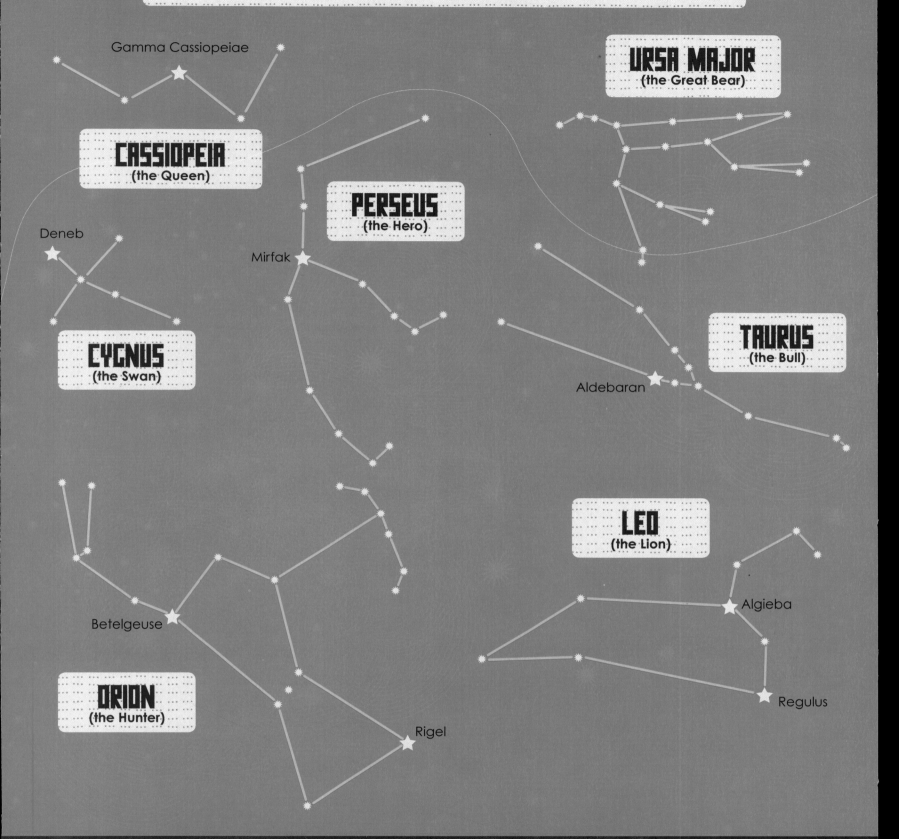

Gamma Cassiopeiae

URSA MAJOR
(the Great Bear)

CASSIOPEIA
(the Queen)

PERSEUS
(the Hero)

Deneb

Mirfak

CYGNUS
(the Swan)

TAURUS
(the Bull)

Aldebaran

LEO
(the Lion)

Algieba

Betelgeuse

Regulus

ORION
(the Hunter)

Rigel

SATUR

1978   1979   1980   1981   1982

Nov – VOYAGER 1 – arrives at Saturn   12 April – first space shuttle launch   1 March –
                                       25 Aug – VOYAGER 2 – arrives at Saturn   VENERA 2 – lan
                                                                                  on Venus

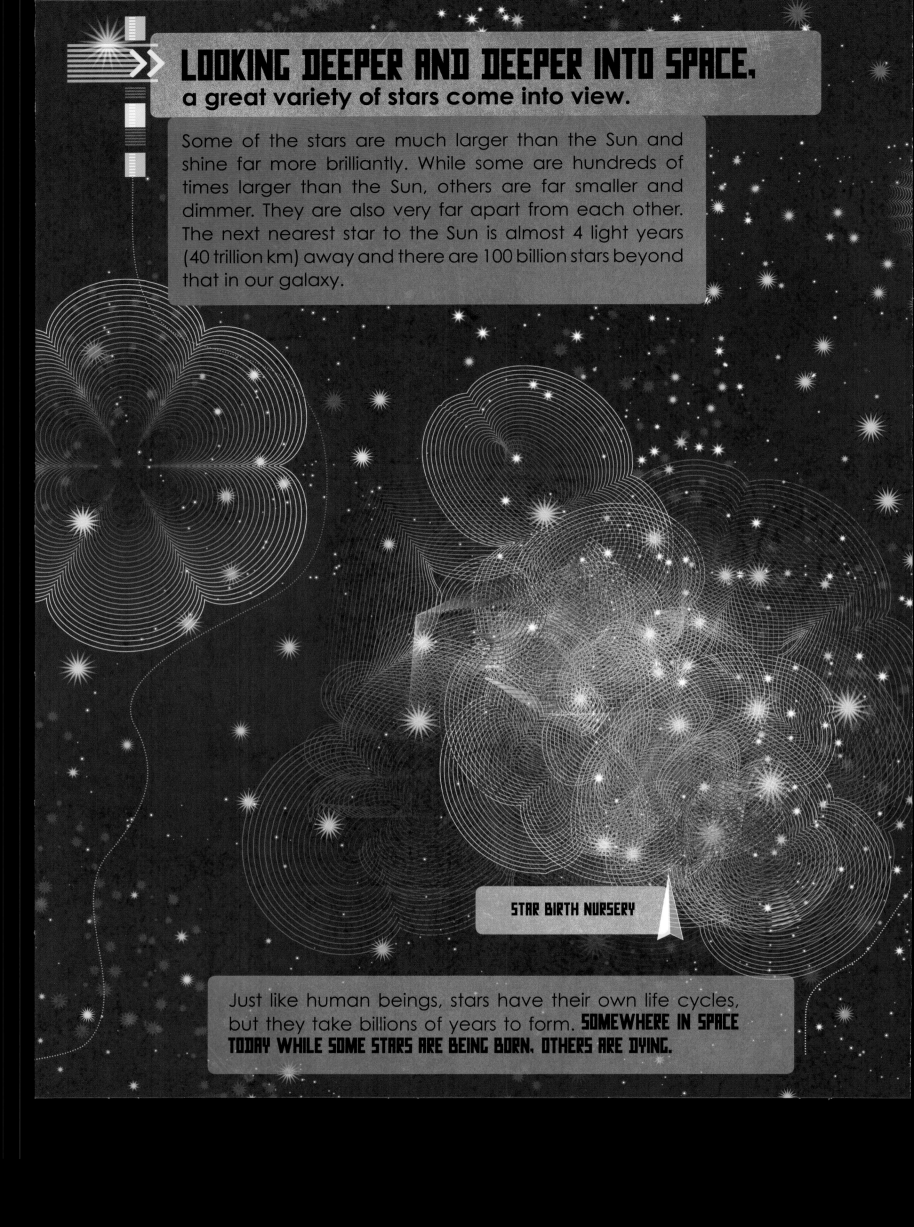

LOOKING DEEPER AND DEEPER INTO SPACE,

a great variety of stars come into view.

Some of the stars are much larger than the Sun and shine far more brilliantly. While some are hundreds of times larger than the Sun, others are far smaller and dimmer. They are also very far apart from each other. The next nearest star to the Sun is almost 4 light years (40 trillion km) away and there are 100 billion stars beyond that in our galaxy.

STAR BIRTH NURSERY

Just like human beings, stars have their own life cycles, but they take billions of years to form. SOMEWHERE IN SPACE TODAY WHILE SOME STARS ARE BEING BORN, OTHERS ARE DYING.

SUPERNOVA

Stars are born in huge clouds of gas and dust. We can see stars being born in giant nurseries like the Orion nebula, which is almost 1,500 light years away from us. **Gravity squeezes gas together to make clumps that get hotter and hotter until, at 15 million °C, a star is born when it begins to make its own nuclear energy.** When stars similar to our Sun die, they first puff up to a much larger size, then they blow out gas to make beautiful nebulae.

Some stars are born up to 100 times heavier than our Sun. These massive stars lead much shorter lives. When their nuclear energy begins to run out they bloat up into supergiant stars. The death of these massive stars is a violent and bright explosion called a supernova. Sometimes a black hole is left behind. Nothing, not even light, can escape from the pull of a black hole!

THE STARS

Just like human beings, stars have their own life cycles, but they can shine for billions of years.

LIFE CYCLE OF A STAR

Sun-like star

Red giant

Planetary nebula

White dwarf

Gas cloud

Massive star

Supergiant

Supernova

Black hole

Neutron star

LARGEST AND MOST POWERFUL KNOWN STARS

The **largest known stars** are almost 1,500 times wider than the Sun. Examples of these supergiant stars are **UY Scuti**, **W26** and **KY Cygni** – more than 3 billion Suns would fit inside these enormous stars.

The most **powerful star*** called **R136a1** is 165,000 light years away. It is more than 35 times the mass of the Sun and is 8,700,000 times more powerful than the Sun.

* Here power refers to the total light given off.

BLACK HOLES

A massive object like a star or galaxy in space curves the space around it.

All the mass is squeezed into a tiny volume. Space is now so curved that matter cannot escape.

1974
March – MARINER 10 – first spacecraft fly-by of Mercury

1975

1976
20 July – VIKING 1 – first pictures from the surface of Mars

1977
Aug–Sept – VOYAGER 1 and 2 – first spacecraft launched to outer solar system

There may be **100,000,000,000 STARS** in our galaxy!
There may be 15 billion Earth-like planets too.

ALL SORTS OF GALAXIES

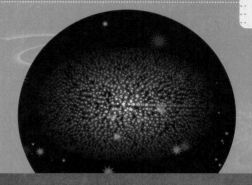

ELLIPTICAL GALAXIES
Ball- and egg-shaped

SPIRAL GALAXIES
Disc with bulge in centre
and spiral arms

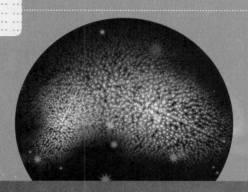

IRREGULARS
No clear shape

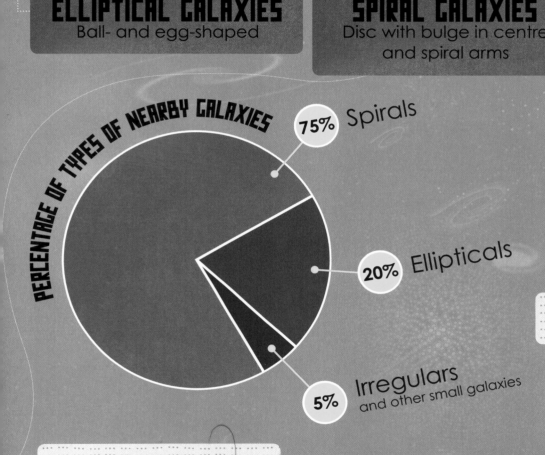

PERCENTAGE OF TYPES OF NEARBY GALAXIES

75% Spirals

20% Ellipticals

5% Irregulars
and other small galaxies

5 million light years

LARGEST GALAXY

Largest known galaxy **IC 1101** is
over 5 million light years across –
more that 50 Milky Way galaxies
could fit across it.

NEAREST GALAXY

The next nearest large spiral galaxy to the Milky Way is called the
Andromeda galaxy. It is the most distant thing we can see with our
naked eyes – but you need a very dark site, and clear night! Andromeda
is **2.3 light years away from Earth** – but it's heading towards us!
The two galaxies will COLLIDE in about 4 billion years!

— JUPITER

969
0 July – APOLLO 11 – Neil
rmstrong – first man to
valk on the Moon

1970
17 Nov – LUNOKHOD 1 – first
unmanned rover on the Moon
15 Dec – VENERA 7 – first probe to
soft-land on the surface of Venus

1971

1972
Dec – APOLLO 17 – last human
mission to the Moon

1973
May – SKYLAB – first
space station starts
being built

ALMOST ALL STARS IN THE UNIVERSE BELONG TO GALAXIES.

The Universe has more than 100 billion galaxies, with each galaxy containing around 100 billion stars, and probably billions of planets too. It takes a gigantic universe to fit in all this matter and still leave huge empty regions of space between them! Looking millions of light years away we can see galaxies everywhere.

Some galaxies are *BEAUTIFUL SPIRALS*;

Most of the galaxies in the Universe exist in groups, bound together by the force of gravity. Our galaxy is part of a local group of about 50 galaxies. Sometimes galaxies in a group get too close and smash into each other. These powerful cosmic collisions can make larger galaxies and lots of new stars.

others are shaped like **SPHERES** or **ELLIPSES**.

On an even larger scale, we can see that different groups of galaxies are also tied together by gravity. Our local group of galaxies is linked with many others to form a supercluster of hundreds of galaxies that stretch 100 million light years across. Looking as far as 300 million light years into space we can see other superclusters made up of thousands of galaxies.

A ZOO OF GALAXIES

OUR POSITION IN OUR GALAXY

SOLAR SYSTEM

SUPERMASSIVE BLACK HOLE

LIGHT YEAR DISTANCES

Light year = distance travelled by light in a year = 9,460,000,000,000 km (9.5 trillion km)

Light moves at a speed of 300,000 km per second!

The Sun takes **220 MILLION YEARS** to complete one orbit around the galaxy.

ASTEROID BELT

1965
18 March – first spacewalk
July – MARINER 4 – first close-up views of Mars

1966
3 Feb – LUNA 9 – first unmanned probe to land on the Moon

1967
Oct – VENERA 4 – first probe to Venus

1968

Here are some theories of what might happen to the Universe in the far future.

CRUNCH

It would stop expanding in the future and start to shrink down.

CONTINUE FOREVER

It would carry on slowly expanding forever.

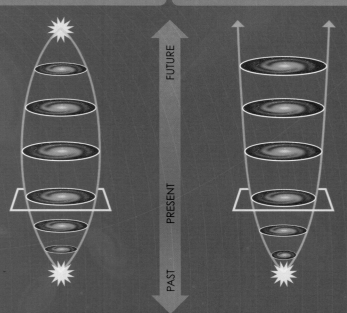

FUTURE

PRESENT

PAST

RUNAWAY UNIVERSE

Today we think that the Universe is expanding more and more quickly.

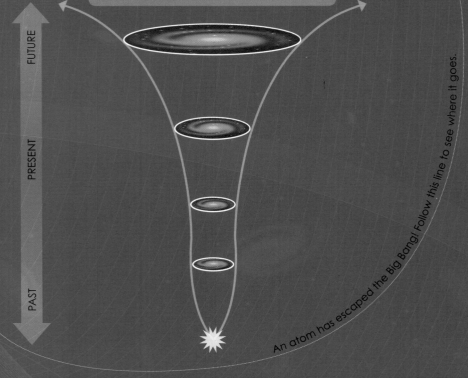

FUTURE

PRESENT

PAST

An atom has escaped the Big Bang! Follow this line to see where it goes.

COSMIC CALENDAR

Imagine the **13.8-billion-year history of the Universe** scaled down to one calendar year.

JANUARY	**1ST**	Big Bang
FEBRUARY		
MARCH		
APRIL		
MAY	**1ST**	Milky Way galaxy forms
JUNE		
JULY		
AUGUST		
SEPTEMBER	**9TH**	Origin of the solar system
	14TH	Earth forms
OCTOBER		
NOVEMBER	**15TH**	First life cells on Earth
DECEMBER	**19TH**	First land plants appear on Ea
	25TH	First dinosaurs
	29TH	Dinosaurs wiped out by comet crash

The last 20 seconds of the year are all of human civilization

EARTH   **MARS**

1961
12 April – VOSTOK 1 – Yuri Gagarin is first man into space

1962

1963
16 June – Valentina Tereshkova is the first woman in space

1964

AT THE EDGE OF THE UNIVERSE WE CAN SEE BACK IN TIME TO ITS VERY BEGINNING.

The Universe began in a Big Bang about 13.8 billion years ago. It started as an incredibly hot and dense bubble thousands of times smaller than a pinhead! Time, space and matter all began with the Big Bang, though we don't know what caused it.

VERY QUICKLY THE UNIVERSE STARTED TO GROW – AND IT IS STILL EXPANDING TODAY.

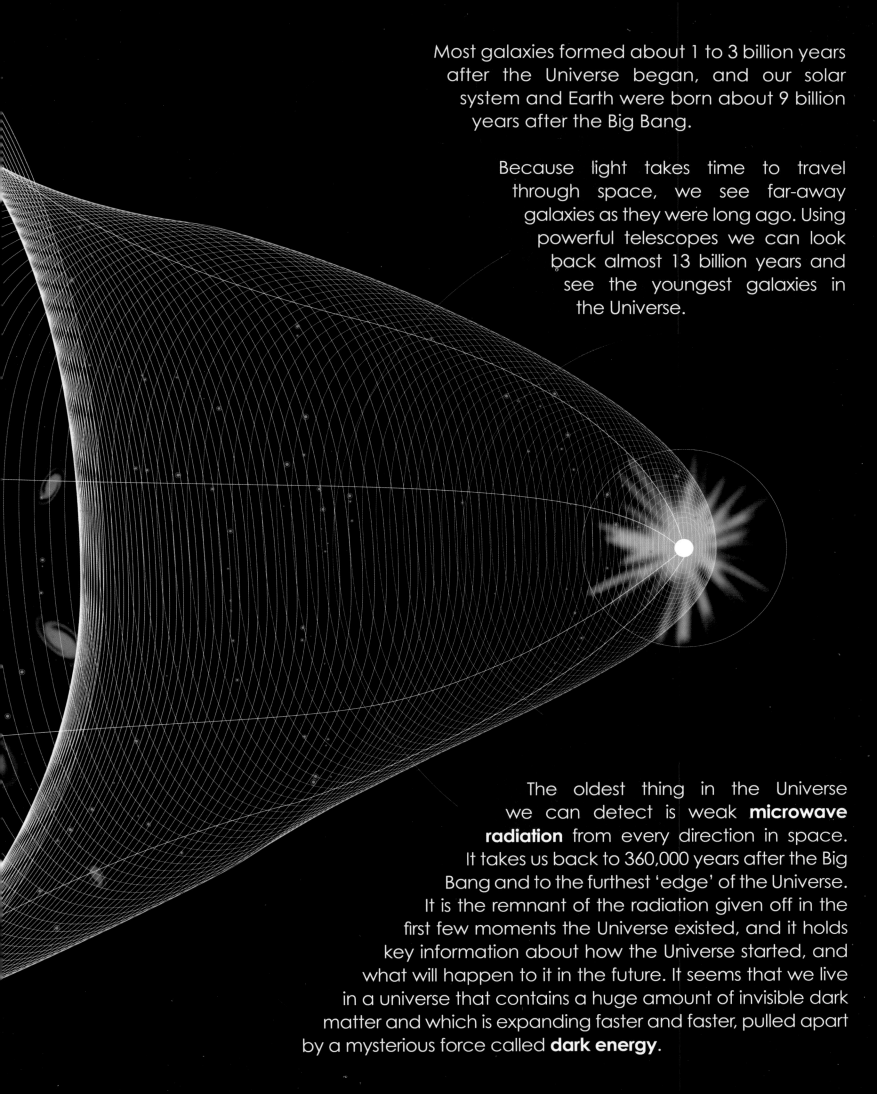

Most galaxies formed about 1 to 3 billion years after the Universe began, and our solar system and Earth were born about 9 billion years after the Big Bang.

Because light takes time to travel through space, we see far-away galaxies as they were long ago. Using powerful telescopes we can look back almost 13 billion years and see the youngest galaxies in the Universe.

The oldest thing in the Universe we can detect is weak **microwave radiation** from every direction in space. It takes us back to 360,000 years after the Big Bang and to the furthest 'edge' of the Universe. It is the remnant of the radiation given off in the first few moments the Universe existed, and it holds key information about how the Universe started, and what will happen to it in the future. It seems that we live in a universe that contains a huge amount of invisible dark matter and which is expanding faster and faster, pulled apart by a mysterious force called **dark energy**.

THE EDGE OF THE UNIVERSE

RUNAWAY UNIVERSE PUSHED APART BY DARK ENERGY

BIG BANG
13.8 billion years ago

AFTERGLOW
380,000 years ago

FIRST STARS FORMED
550 million years ago

GALAXIES FORMED WITH STARS AND PLANETS

THE UNIVERSE IS MADE OF:

5%
Ordinary matter
Stars, galaxies, planets, dust and gas

24%
Cold dark matter
Made of mysterious particles much smaller than an atom

71%
Dark energy
A mysterious force that is making the Universe expand faster and faster

---

SCALE MODEL OF OUR SOLAR SYSTEM

THE SUN — — MERCURY — — VENUS

TIMELINE OF HUMAN SPACE EXPLORATION

1957
4 Oct – SPUTNIK 1 – first artificial satellite in space
3 Nov – SPUTNIK 2 – first live animal (Laika the dog) in space

1958

1959
Sept–Oct – LUNA missions – first probes to the Moon

1960